WORSHIP CLASSICS
FOR UKULELE

ISBN 978-1-5400-5138-7

Visit Hal Leonard Online at
www.halleonard.com

Contact us:
Hal Leonard
7777 West Bluemound Road
Milwaukee, WI 53213
Email: info@halleonard.com

In Europe, contact:
Hal Leonard Europe Limited
42 Wigmore Street
Marylebone, London, W1U 2RN
Email: info@halleonardeurope.com

In Australia, contact:
Hal Leonard Australia Pty. Ltd.
4 Lentara Court
Cheltenham, Victoria, 3192 Australia
Email: info@halleonard.com.au

Agnus Dei

Words and Music by Michael W. Smith

All Who Are Thirsty

Words and Music by Brenton Brown and Glenn Robertson

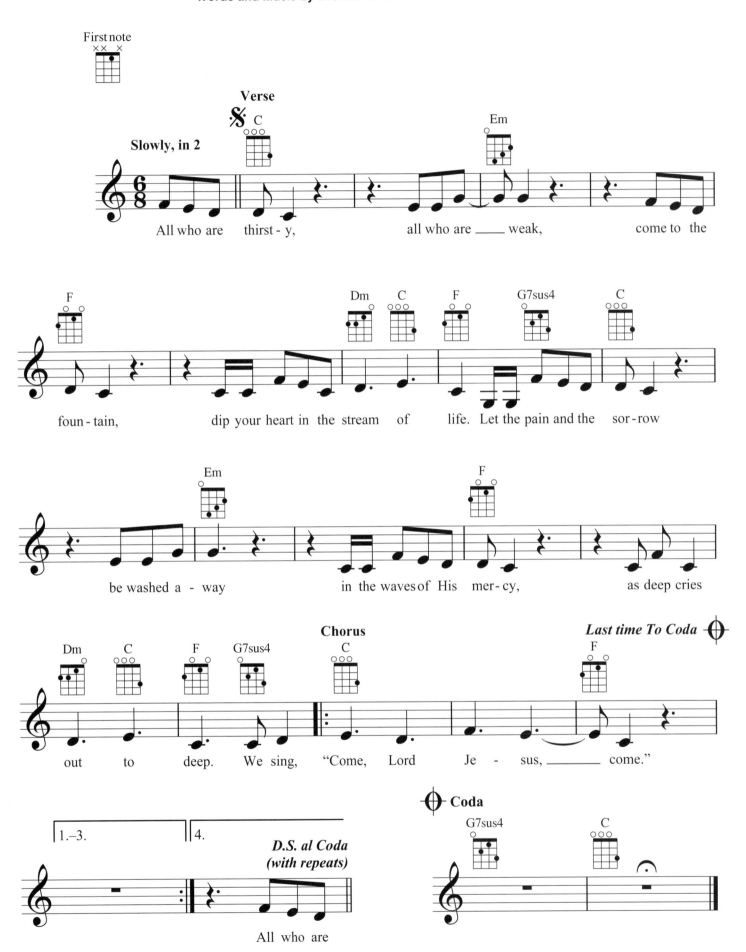

As the Deer

Words and Music by Martin Nystrom

Awesome God

Words and Music by Rich Mullins

Better Is One Day

Words and Music by Matt Redman

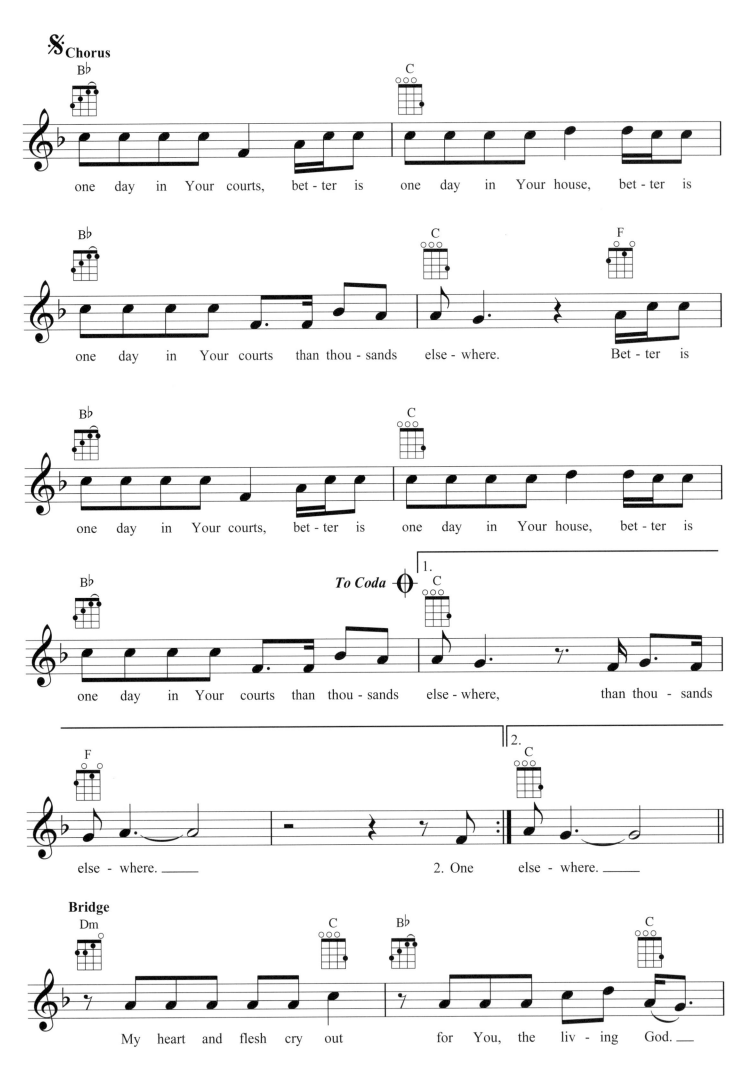

Your Spir-it's wa-ter to my soul. ____ I've tast-ed and I've seen,

come once a-gain to me. _ I will draw near to You, I will draw near to You. _

Pre-Chorus

____ Bet-ter is one day, ____ bet-ter is

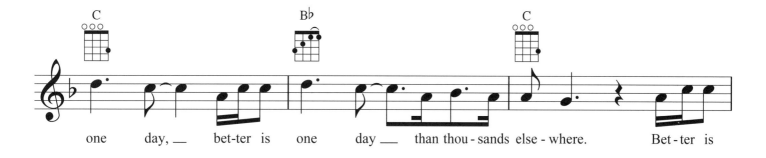

one day, ____ bet-ter is one day ___ than thou-sands else-where. Bet-ter is

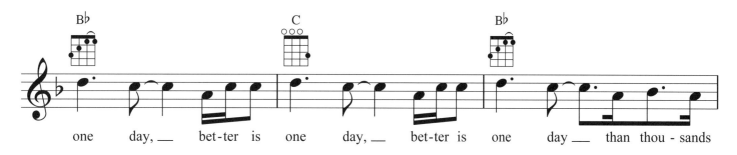

one day, ____ bet-ter is one day, ____ bet-ter is one day ___ than thou-sands

⊕ **Coda**

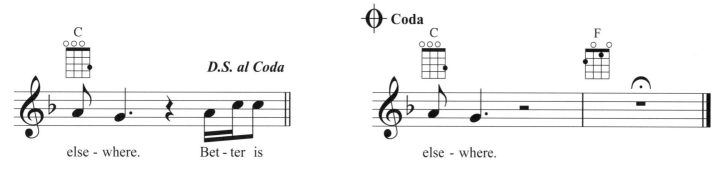

D.S. al Coda

else-where. Bet-ter is

else-where.

Be Unto Your Name

Words and Music by Lynn DeShazo and Gary Sadler

Chorus

high. _____ }
name. _____ }

Ho - ly, ho - ly,

Lord God Al - might - y. Wor - thy

is the Lamb who was slain. High - est

prais - es, hon - or and glo - ry be un -

to Your name, _____ be un -

to Your name. _____

Breathe

Words and Music by Marie Barnett

Change My Heart Oh God

Words and Music by Eddie Espinosa

Draw Me Close

Words and Music by Kelly Carpenter

to feel the warmth _ of Your _ em - brace. _

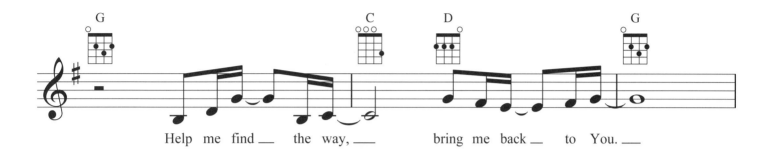

Help me find _ the way, _ bring me back _ to You. _

Chorus

You're all _ I want, _

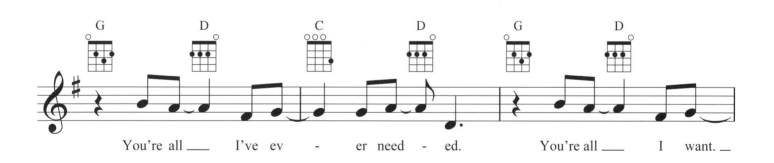

You're all _ I've ev - er need - ed. You're all _ I want. _

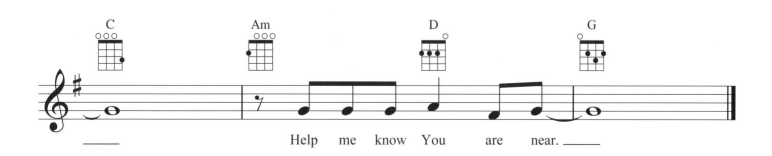

_ Help me know You are near. _

Give Us Clean Hands

Words and Music by Charlie Hall

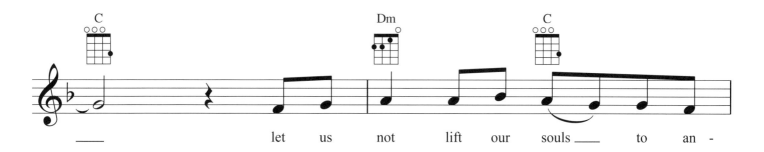

let us not lift our souls ____ to an -

Chorus 2

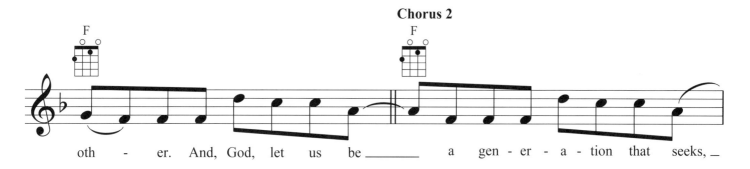

oth - er. And, God, let us be _____ a gen - er - a - tion that seeks, _

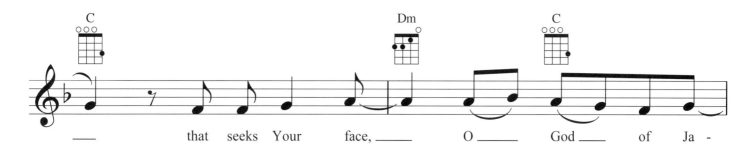

____ that seeks Your face, _____ O _____ God _____ of Ja -

- cob. And, God, let us be _____ a gen - er - a - tion that seeks, _

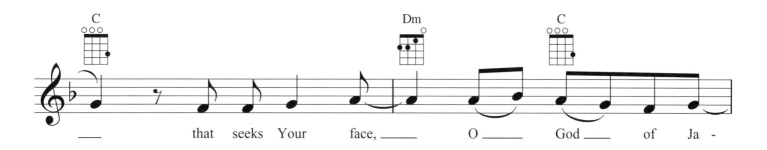

____ that seeks Your face, _____ O _____ God _____ of Ja -

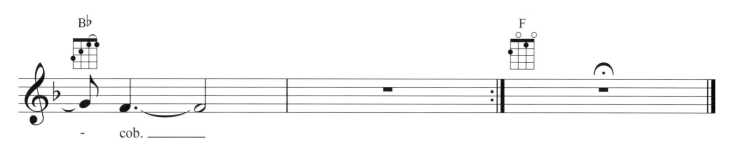

- cob. _____

Glorify Thy Name

Words and Music by Donna W. Adkins

He Has Made Me Glad
(I Will Enter His Gates)

Words and Music by Leona Von Brethorst

He Is Exalted

Words and Music by Twila Paris

First note

Verse
Flowing, in 2

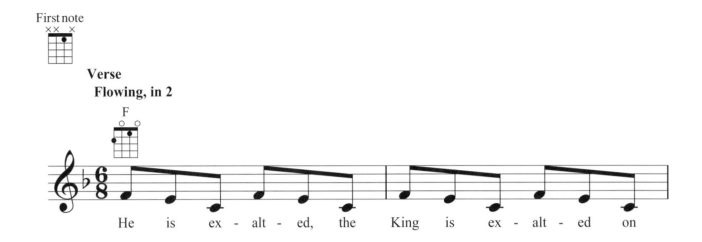

He is ex - alt - ed, the King is ex - alt - ed on

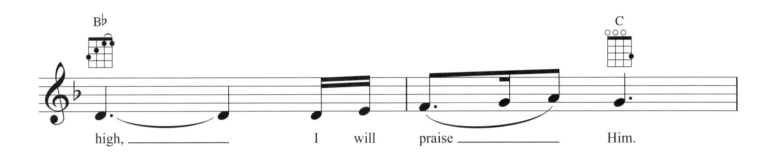

high, _____ I will praise _____ Him.

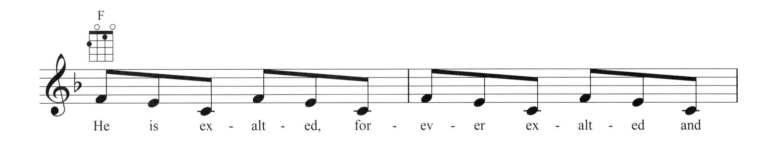

He is ex - alt - ed, for - ev - er ex - alt - ed and

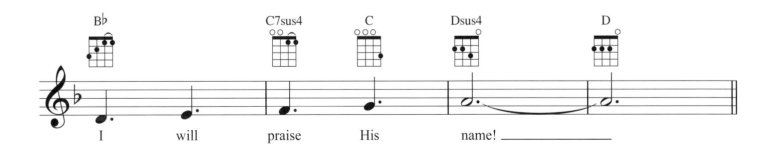

I will praise His name! _____

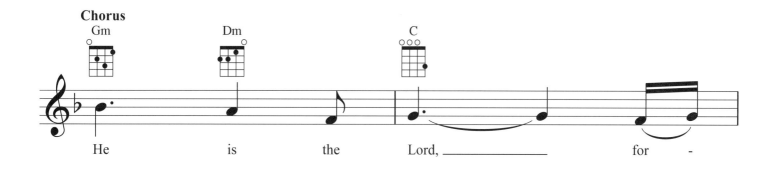

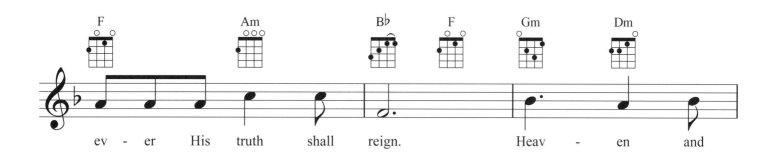

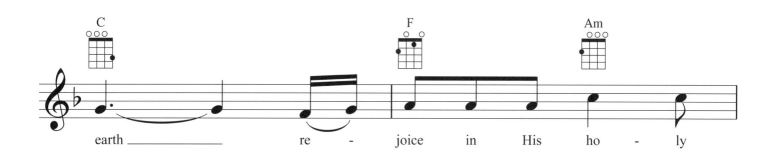

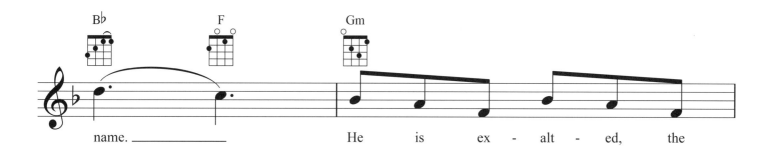

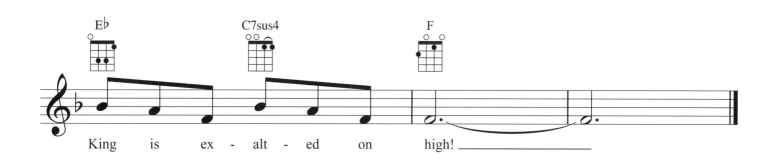

He Knows My Name

Words and Music by Tommy Walker

I Love You Lord

Words and Music by Laurie Klein

I Could Sing of Your Love Forever

Words and Music by Martin Smith

Jesus, Name Above All Names

Words and Music by Naida Hearn

Sanctuary

Words and Music by John Thompson and Randy Scruggs

Lamb of God

Words and Music by Twila Paris

Chorus

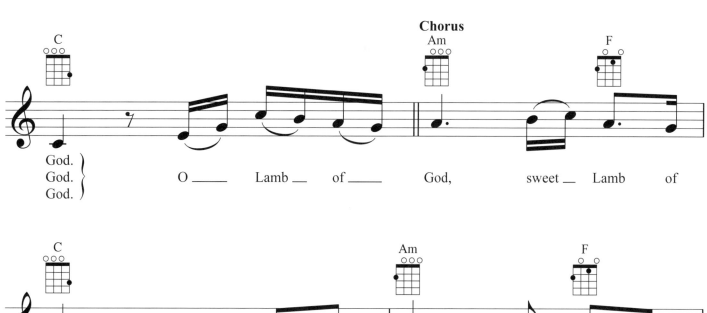

God.
God.
God.

O ___ Lamb ___ of ___ God, sweet ___ Lamb of

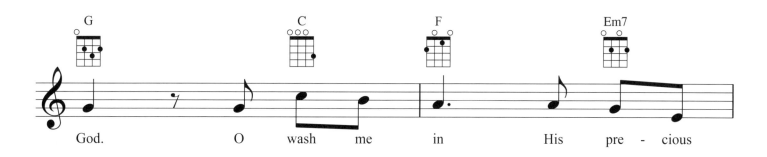

God; I love the ho - ly Lamb of

God. O wash me in His pre - cious

blood, (1., 2.) my Je - sus Christ, the Lamb of
(3.) till I am just a lamb of

1., 2. | 3.

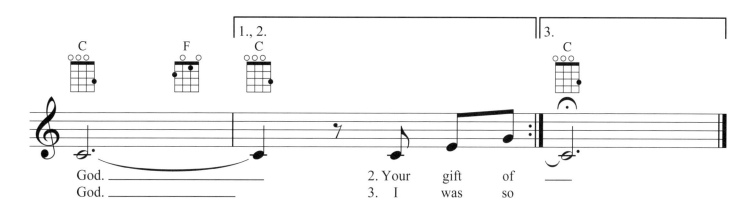

God. ___ 2. Your gift of ___
God. ___ 3. I was so

31

Majesty

Words and Music by Jack Hayford

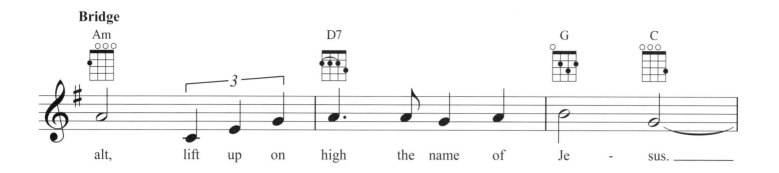

alt, lift up on high the name of Je - sus. _____

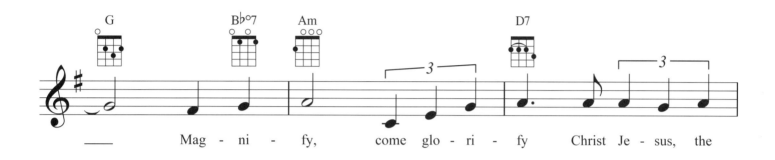

_____ Mag - ni - fy, come glo - ri - fy Christ Je - sus, the

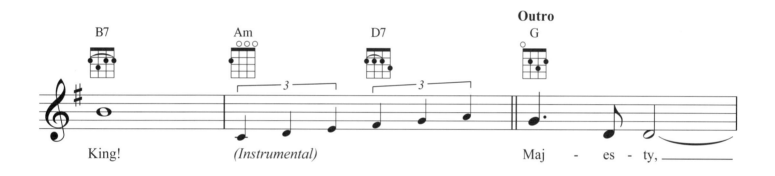

King! *(Instrumental)* Maj - es - ty, _____

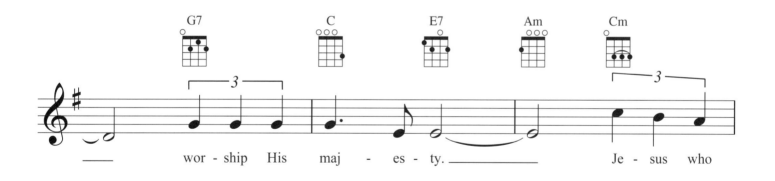

_____ wor - ship His maj - es - ty. _____ Je - sus who

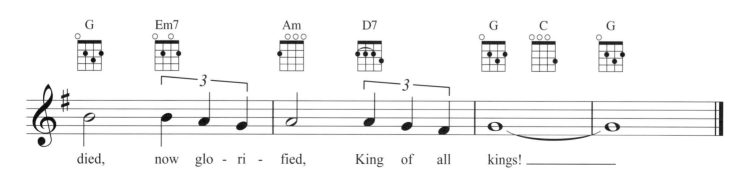

died, now glo - ri - fied, King of all kings! _____

Seek Ye First

Words and Music by Karen Lafferty

There Is a Redeemer

Words and Music by Melody Green

Shine, Jesus, Shine

Words and Music by Graham Kendrick

Shine on ___ me, shine on ___ me.

Chorus

Shine, Je - sus, shine, ___ fill this land with the Fa - ther's glo - ry. Blaze, Spir - it, blaze, ___ set our hearts on fire. Flow, riv - er, flow, ___ flood the na - tions with grace and mer - cy. Send forth Your Word, ___ Lord, and let there be light.

Trading My Sorrows

Words and Music by Darrell Evans

yes, yes, Lord. _ Yes, Lord, yes, Lord, yes, yes, Lord, A - men. _

Bridge

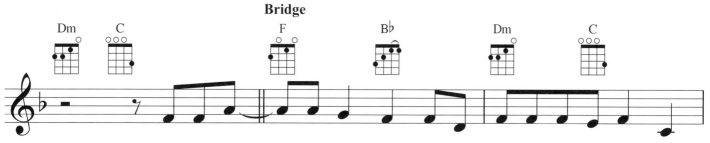

I am pressed _ but not crushed, per - se - cut - ed, not a - ban - doned,

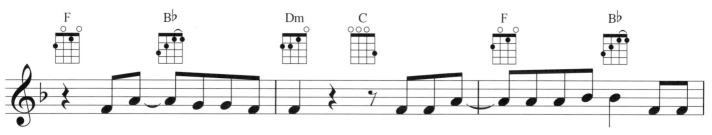

struck down _ but not de - stroyed. I am blessed _ be-yond the curse, for His

prom - ise will en - dure, that His joy is gon - na be my strength. _

_ Though the sor - row _ may last for _ the night, His joy _

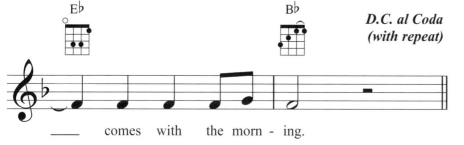

_ comes with the morn - ing.

D.C. al Coda
(with repeat)

Coda

_

This Is the Day

Words and Music by Les Garrett